For Mom & Dad !

Kids Can Press acknowledges the financial support of the Government of Ontario, through the Ontario Media Development Corporation's Ontario Book Initiative; the Ontario Arts Council; the Canada Council for the Arts; and the Government of Canada, through the BPIDP, for our publishing activity.

Published in Canada by
Kids Can Press Ltd.
25 Dockside Drive
Toronto, ON M5A 0B5

Published in the U.S. by
Kids Can Press Ltd.
2250 Military Road
Tonawanda, NY 14150

www.kidscanpress.com

The artwork in this book was rendered with pencil, watercolor, copy paper, elephant poop paper and digital magic.

The text is set in Rockwell, Jerky Tash and Rumpelstiltskin.

Edited by Tara Walker
Designed by Ben Clanton and Rachel Di Salle

This book is smyth sewn casebound.
Manufactured in Singapore, in 10/2011 by Tien Wah Press (Pte) Ltd.

CM 12 0 9 8 7 6 5 4 3 2 1

Library and Archives Canada Cataloguing in Publication

Clanton, Ben, 1988–
    Vote for me! / by Ben Clanton.

ISBN 978-1-55453-822-5

    I. Title.

PZ7.C523Vo 2012   j813'.6   C2011-905524-4

Kids Can Press is a corus™ Entertainment company

Hey, you!
Yes, YOU with the great hair and that dazzling smile.
Listen, you should—

* In fact, 97% of sheep agree that Donkey is #1. (The other 3% are the black sheep of their families.)

Not to change the subject, BUT I've got a question I've been meaning to ask you. Do you like CANDY?
Because . . . if you vote for ME, I'll give you a sucker!

NUTS?!
My Uncle Sam is allergic to nuts!
  Speaking of family . . .

As it turns out, I know your friend's
mother's aunt's gym teacher's pastor's
duck-billed platypus.

  So, we're practically FAMILY,
    and you've GOT to vote for family.

Forget the elephant in the room. He's just jealous . . .

of this redonkulously AWESOME list of reasons why YOU should pick me!

Reasons to vote for ME!

1. I'M #1.

2. CANDY!

3. I'm family!

4. I wear CLEAN UNDIES.

6. My mommy says you should!

7. I know where you sleep.

yada yada yada yada

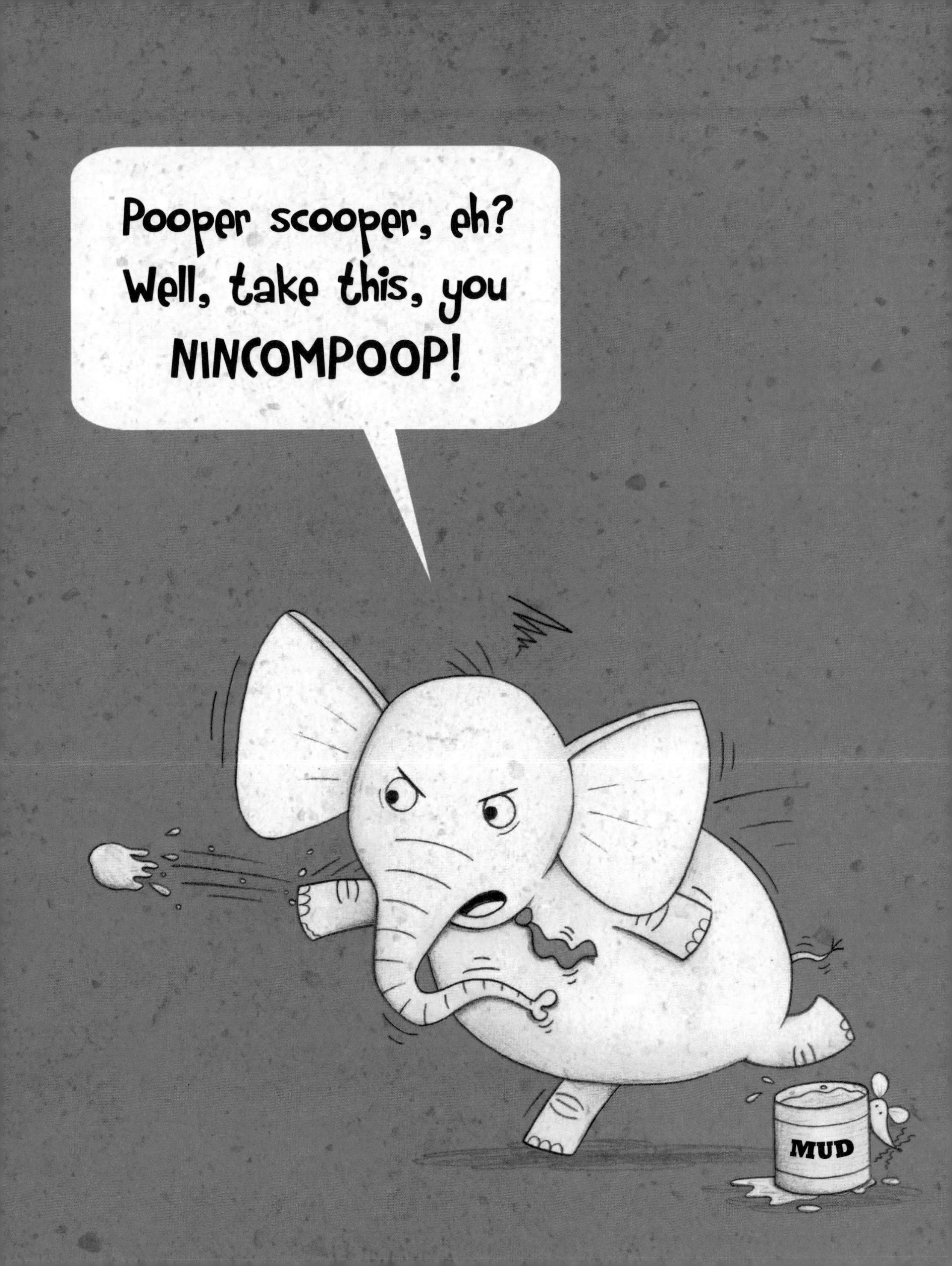
Pooper scooper, eh? Well, take this, you NINCOMPOOP!
MUD

OAF!

Dim-witted dolt!

SMELLYPANTS!

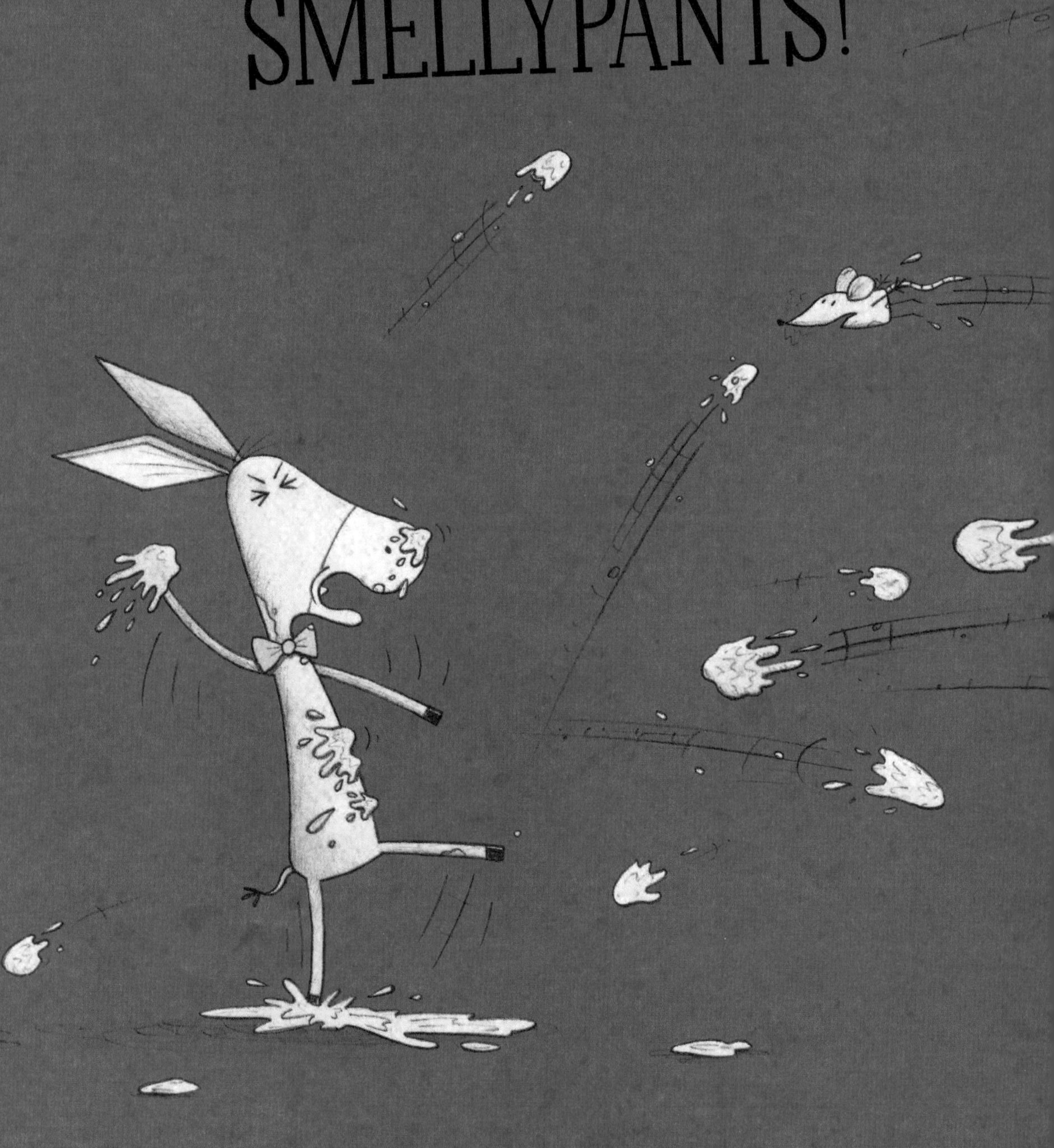

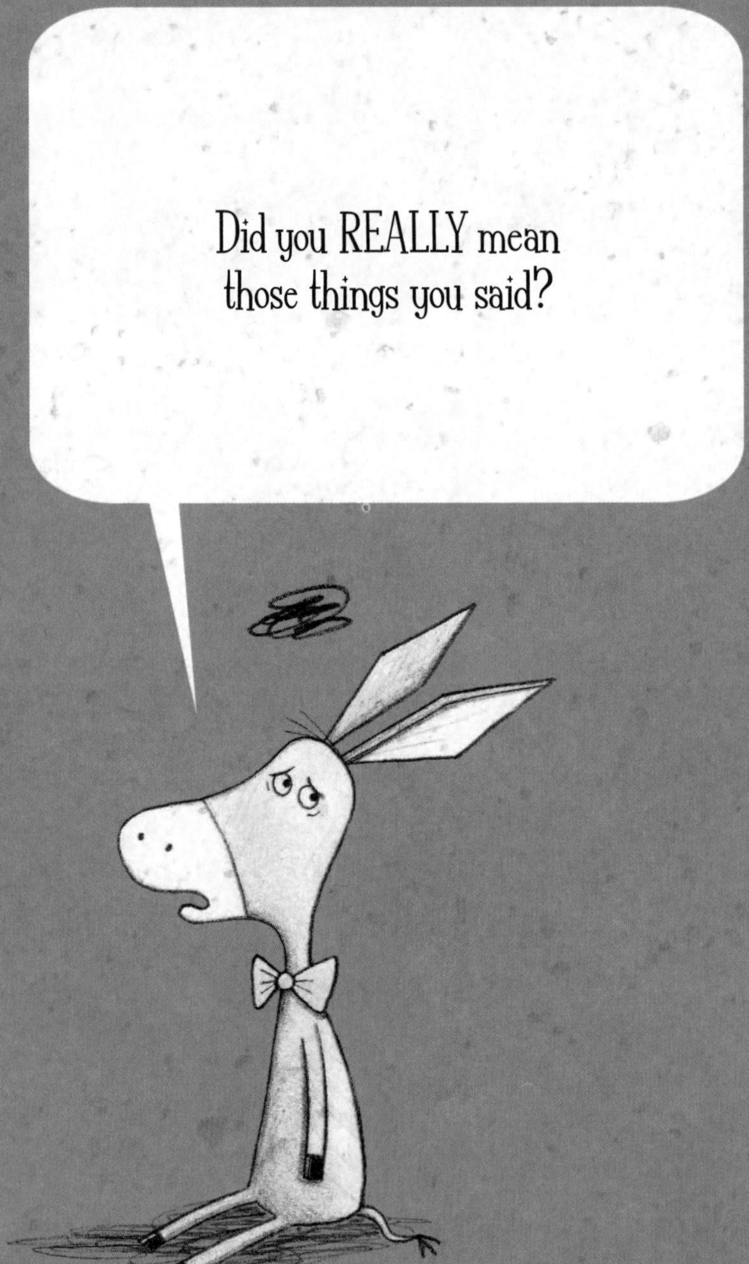
Did you REALLY mean those things you said?

Well, even though Elephant and I are friends now, YOU still need to pick just one of us.
So, WHO do YOU want to vote for?
Go ahead and SHOUT IT OUT!

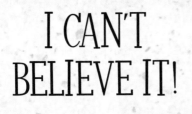

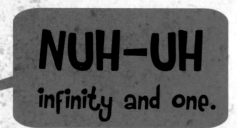

NUH-UH infinity and one.

Well, YUH-HUH one more than whatever you say next and there is nothing more, so that is

THE END.